Budd

Susan Ring

Illustrated by Twila Schofield

Rigby®

A Harcourt Achieve Imprint

www.Rigby.com
1-800-531-5015

It was a very
warm day.
"I'm hot," said Danny.

"What can we do?"
asked Dawn.

3

"We can give Buddy a bath!" said Danny.

"What a good idea," said Dawn.

So Danny and Dawn
went into the house.

They came out
with a big tub.
They put it
on the grass.

6

Then they got
some soap.
They put it
in the tub.

Then they got
the hose.
They put water
in the tub.

Dawn said, "Now we have a tub, soap, and water."

"But we do not have Buddy!" said Danny.

Dawn said, "Come
here Buddy."
But Buddy ran away!

Buddy did not stop.
So Danny and Dawn
ran, too.

"You need to get in the tub!" said Danny.

So Buddy jumped
in the tub.

Then they all got
a bath!